Permission requests should be submitted in writing to
tracey@daringwomanmedia.com

For ordering information, special discount for bulk
purchases, or to request Tracey speak for your group,
contact mea@daringwomanmedia.com

Printed in the United States of America

First Printing, 2016
Second Edition, 2017

ISBN 1530346320
ISBN-13: 978-1530346325

Daring Woman Media, Inc.
457 Nathan Dean Blvd.
Suite 105-109
Dallas, GA 30132

www.DaringWomanMedia.com

thank you

There have been some very special people who have helped me on my journey to writing this book. Too numerous to name everyone and my thanks goes out to each and every one of them.

Here are a few special thanks that must be said:

To my husband, Mark, I am so grateful for your love and support through the good times and bad. Thank you for believing in me when I didn't believe in myself.

To Roger, you were with me in the beginning and through the biggest part of my journey. Thank you for being there to fall back on when the going got tough, and never giving up on the belief that I could be a success.

To my children, I know there have been a lot of long hours, a lot of sacrifice on your part. Thank you for loving me when I was cranky, overwhelmed and stressed out beyond belief. It was for you that I began this journey.

To the coaches, mentors, friends over the years, I love you all. Thank you for being there, supporting me and reminding me that I do know what I'm doing when self-doubt crept in.

Most of all, thank you Kimberly Jackson. Without your advice on that November day sitting in Starbucks, I'd have never begun my journey and I wouldn't be writing this today. I will always be grateful for you.

TABLE OF CONTENTS

CHAPTER 1

HOW I BEGAN MY JOURNEY

I began my journey into entrepreneurialism when I was 18. My first attempt was selling Avon. I was my best customer.

Years later, I bought a failing gas station with the hopes of providing a solid income for my family. I blindly entered into a partnership and because my partner (the financier) didn't want to hire an attorney from the onset, we lost thousands of dollars due to a shady deal with the landlord. I only purchased the name/products. Not the property.

Two more babies later, I started an in-home daycare. That didn't last long either.

What I learned was there is a ton of hard work that goes into building your own business. It takes far more than hanging out your shingle and waiting for the hordes of customers to flock to you and buy your products or services.

Fast forward, I am now a successful entrepreneur of 10 years.

Starting a virtual business is an entirely different venture than working in a brick and mortar business. The world is truly your oyster.

I remember the day I decided to become a Virtual Assistant as clearly as if it were yesterday.

It was November 17, 2007. I was having coffee with a good friend and business coach.

I'm not talking about your run of the mill coach either. She's the kind that works with people like CEO's of fortune 500 companies. Guys like Brian Tracy and Jack Canfield know her well. So, when she gave me advice, I listened.

We were sitting in the Starbucks area of Barnes and Noble and I was complaining yet again about how much I was really beginning to hate my job. I was the vice president of a small, accounts receivable financing company.

While it sounds glamorous, the truth is, it wasn't. I was really VP in title only. The salary I earned did not measure up to all the work I did. I was a secretary, business development officer and sales person all in one.

I became the face of the company...the one everyone knew at the networking meetings. I was dubbed the Queen of Networking in Atlanta because I was so well known. A fact which later helped me as I began my new journey.

As we sat and talked about my misery, she brought up some good points. I was very strong in the administrative field. I was well-liked and respected by my peers, and I was always asking how I could help others. She suggested that I start a Virtual Assistant company.

Back then, nobody knew what a Virtual Assistant (or VA) was. It was a blossoming industry full of promise, mystery and very little guidance.
I spent the rest of the day on the internet trying to figure out what a VA really was. What did they do? How did this work? There wasn't much to go on.

I found some basic info. The International Virtual Assistant Association (IVAA) was newly formed as well as A Clayton's Secretary (an Australian based company run by a respected VA, Kathie Thomas).

From those websites, I was able to get a glimpse into the world of becoming a Virtual Assistant.

By Monday, I had a website and my first go at a VA business was born...Your Virtual Round To-it. A name nobody understood but I thought was clever. It was a start.

I started out working on my VA business after my J O B hours, on my lunch hour and on weekends. I began telling a few key networkers about my new endeavor and by April of 2008 I was a full-time VA.

Starting out, I did tasks such as running errands for people, helping organize offices and even "babysitting" them while they worked (some people just need that accountability to get things done).

I'll never forget sitting at a client's house covering her patio chairs with thick plastic vinyl to prepare them for winter and thinking, "This was not what I had in mind."

I was still away from home too much and that was one of the reasons I wanted to stop working an actual job in the first place. I missed my family. My kids needed me home.

It was time to change tactics. I found that in-person networking ate up too much of my time as well. So, I turned to the social networks.

I spent hours on Twitter talking, building relationships and making connections. In 2008 I was named one of the Top 50 Most Powerful and Influential Women in Social Media.

My business was growing as I made new connections through social media and I was learning so many new things.

For several years I was content earning about $35,000 a year. My then husband made a decent living as a truck driver and I only needed to supplement our income.

In 2012, my world changed. My best friend was killed in a single car tragic accident. I spiraled downward into a deep depression and all but shut my business down and focused everything on the animal rescue we had just started the month before she died.

6 months later, the fog began to clear and I made some major life changes. I closed the rescue and ended my 12-year marriage. I was now the sole support for my children.

It was time to take my business seriously and no longer think of it as a hobby job. In 2013, I earned a measly $15,000 for the entire year.

I stepped up my game, expanded my virtual team, hired a business coach (even though I couldn't afford it) and tripled my income in 2014. By 2015 I had broken the 6-figure mark.

I have hired several assistants over the years. I've rebranded 3 times. I figured out why I was dropping balls, where the careless errors came from.

I learned what it takes to go from $15,000 a year to 6-figures.

I've wanted to write this book for years. Deep down inside, I knew I wasn't ready to pass on my knowledge just yet. I still had much to learn before I was ready to help new VAs become successful.

I needed to reach my own personal level of success before I felt I was ready to help others. This book has been almost a decade in the making. It's been an amazing journey filled with laughter, tears, love, heartache, joy and success. A journey I wouldn't trade for the world.

My goal with this book is to give you the steps and tools you need to begin your journey to Becoming a VA and gain the skillset to conquer the Virtual Assistant industry.

I wish you the best of luck and the most success,

CHAPTER 2

WHAT IS A VIRTUAL ASSISTANT ANYWAY?

There is a lot of misconception around the Virtual Assistant industry. The term Virtual Assistant is fast becoming an umbrella term for anyone who works remotely and assists others.

But what truly is a Virtual Assistant? What do they do? How does this work?

By definition, a Virtual Assistant is a business owner who supports others remotely as an independent contractor. A Virtual Assistant can be administrative, technical and/or creative in nature.

The term Virtual Assistant (or VA) is widely being used as a catch-all for anyone who supports other entrepreneurs remotely. Because of this, new VAs are confused and unclear as to what exactly a Virtual Assistant does or can do.

TYPES OF VIRTUAL ASSISTANTS

There are two main categories of Virtual Assistants. Anything outside of these two categories is a specialization and not truly what a Virtual Assistant is, but what they can become.

GENERAL VIRTUAL ASSISSTANT - A General Virtual Assistant (often referred to as a General VA or a GVA) is usually where a new VA starts. The skills you acquire from years as an administrative professional can be well used as a General VA.

General VAs can provide support to a wide variety **of professionals** such as CEOs, lawyers, business owners and other entrepreneurs.

TASKS ROUTINELY PERFORMED BY A GENERAL VA CONSISTS OF:

- ◇ Email management
- ◇ Scheduling
- ◇ Travel arrangements
- ◇ Gatekeeper
- ◇ Minor editing
- ◇ Creating word documents
- ◇ Creating spreadsheets
- ◇ Creating PowerPoints
- ◇ Simple newsletters
- ◇ Scheduling prewritten social media content
- ◇ Maintaining an online calendar
- ◇ Phone calls

PROGRAMS A GENERAL VA SHOULD KNOW OR LEARN:

- ◇ Word
- ◇ Excel
- ◇ PowerPoint
- ◇ Google Docs
- ◇ Google Calendar
- ◇ Various scheduling calendars (Time Trade, Schedule Once, Vcita, Accuity)
- ◇ Constant Contact
- ◇ Mail Chimp
- ◇ Instant Teleseminar
- ◇ Free Conference Call
- ◇ Go to Meeting/Webinar

TECHNICAL VIRTUAL ASSISTANT- A Technical Virtual Assistant (often known as a Tech VA or Techie) provides more in-depth support to their clients.

TASKS ROUTINELY PERFORMED BY A Tech VA CONSISTS OF:

- ◇ Creating opt-in funnels
- ◇ Newsletters
- ◇ E-mail blasts
- ◇ Website maintenance
- ◇ Building sales pages & sales funnels
- ◇ Creating e-mail accounts

⬦ Setting up Google apps
⬦ Google analytics
⬦ Posting Blogs
⬦ Creating campaigns or e-mail lists

PROGRAMS MOST OFTEN USED BY TECH VAS:

⬦ Wordpress
⬦ LeadPages
⬦ ClickFunnels
⬦ Infusionsoft
⬦ Mail Chimp
⬦ Ontraport
⬦ ConvertKit
⬦ Active Campaign
⬦ Shopify
⬦ Google
⬦ Adobe Pro
⬦ Instant Teleseminar
⬦ Go to Meeting/Webinar

THE JACK/JILL OF ALL TRADES – A third category could be the Jack or Jill of All Trades. These VAs have a little knowledge in a lot of areas, but they don't necessarily have strong skills in these areas. They can combine the general VA with the Tech VA and may even have some basic skill sets of the specializations.

In the beginning, most of us become a Jack or Jill of All Trades, at least for a little while as we are learning and growing our skill set.

Just remember the saying, "Jack of all trades, master of none."

While there's nothing wrong with being able to do a little in a lot of areas, the money will come when you can specialize and really focus on one or two areas such as launches or becoming an OBM.

We certainly need the Jack/Jill of All Trades so if you are comfortable in thsi area, by all means, stay there!

SPECIALIZATIONS OFTEN REFERRED TO AS A VIRTUAL ASSISTANT:

ONLINE BUSINESS MANAGER – As they develop their skills and strengths, many VAs transition into the world of online business management. An Online Business Manager (or OBM) takes the knowledge of being a VA and enhances it ten-fold. An OBM becomes a true partner in a client's business.

An OBM must be very detail oriented and incredibly organized. They become the backbone of their client's business. It's their role to run the business much like a Chief Operations OFficer of a large corporation.

The OBM will not only be managing teams, but also managing projects and should know all the sptes and nuances of putting together large, complex launches. They will be watching budgets and making sure the clients aren't throwing money away. They also monitor ROI and should know how to read analytics for many different areas.

I advise working as a VA for a minimum of 2-3 years before learning about becoming an OBM. This will give you the time needed to really learn and grow as a business owner and person.

PROJECT MANAGER – A Project Manager (or PM) is a step below OBM. THey do exactly what the title suggests; manage projects. This can be an ongoing role or project based. Like the OBM, a PM must be very detail oriented and incredibly organized. They must be able to see the big picture and have the ability to break it down into tiny tasks and put it all back together.

They will have most of the same skills and knowledge as an OBM. Most common projects would be building funnels, launches, website builds and telesummits. Until you clearly know all the insa nd outs of these main projects, it would be wise to not try and do it.

WEB DESIGNER – A web designer is often referred to as a Virtual Assistant. While many VAs have web design skills, a true web designer is not a VA, they don't do any other VA type work.

SOCIAL MEDIA MANAGER – Like a web designer, a true social media manager specializes in ONLY social media. They know the ins and outs of growitng your fan base, creating ads that convert and sparking engagement. Social media is much more than just posting content. While a VA can write content and get it online, a true social media manager creates strategies, measures ROI and monitors engagement. They do nothing else but social media.

COPYWRITERS – It takes a special skill to become a valued copywriter. While many VAs can write articles and blog posts, not everyone can write copy that converts. Sales pages, website copy and even email follow-ups need a special knowledge if you want it to convert to sales. Even in the copywriting industry, there are levels. Not all copywriters can create incredible sales copy. And not all sales copywriters can write inspiring blog posts.

Most likely you will begin as a General Admin VA and move on from there. If you already have some of the specialized VA skills, that just gives you a leg up on your competition and a strong beginning toward growth.

CHAPTER 3

WHAT IS YOUR WHY?

What is that one thing that is drawing you to becoming an entrepreneur?

Why do you really want to start your own business?

Money?
Freedom?
Staying home with kids?
Tired of the 9-5 rat race?
Being your own boss?

My passion is helping others. It's what I love to do and it's what I have an affinity for. My strengths have changed over the years, but my passion hasn't. For me, being a Virtual Assistant was like finding my true calling.

My big "WHY" to starting my Virtual Assistant company was so that I could work from home and be there with my kids. I used to be gone before they'd get up for school and come home after they went to bed. Now I'm here all the time. I'm able to see them off to school. I'm here for all their performances, games, parties, etc. I'm able to be a mom again and it's because of my business that I can do that.

But that's not the only reason.

There's something rewarding when, at the end of the day, you can sit back and say this is my success. This business was built with my two hands and look at all the dreams I've helped come true.

At first, I fell into the entrepreneur's trap of thinking that being a business owner meant I'd have more time, more freedom and could work whenever I wanted.

And in some cases, this is true. It certainly is truer for me now than it was in the beginning. But it's not always the case. Especially when you are just starting your own journey.

Remember, you have people who are depending on you to get their work complete and in a timely manner. If you're always having "life issues", your business is going to suffer.

I see new Virtual Assistants who start their business for the wrong reasons, mainly out of desperation. Often, it's based around a drastic life change and they think this will be an easy way to support their family.

They get caught up in the glamour of:

       ⋄ Working from home
       ⋄ Making their own hours
       ⋄ Making decent money
       ⋄ No commuting
       ⋄ Working in pajamas
       ⋄ More family time

A Virtual Assistant is a business owner. With that role comes certain responsibilities and obligations. If you can't get out of the employee mindset, you will never survive as a business owner. It's up to you to make your money now. If you don't work, you don't get paid. It's that simple.

Creating a successful business is hard work. In the beginning, when you are balancing your regular job, building your business and tending to family, your workload is going to double if not triple. Just remember it's temporary. You have a goal and you must work hard for that goal.

An Olympic athlete does not wake up one morning and just become an Olympian. They work incredibly hard and make lots of sacrifices to achieve their dreams. It's the same for you.

This not a "build it and they will come" scenario. That only works in the movies. Building a successful business is going to require time, dedication, sacrifice (for you and others) and a lot of trial and error.

You will not jump into the ring and start making gobs of money. It takes time to build your skills, build your clientele and build your reputation. Be patient. It will happen.

You have to crawl before you can run. I see new VAs who have been in the industry a year or less all of a sudden decide they can be an Online Business Manager (OBM) or a coach.

First off, steer clear of these types. They don't have the knowledge or skills yet for either role. Landing your first client does not give you the skills to coach others.

Secondly, while the money for those roles is great, there's a reason they get paid what they do. They've earned it. They've put in the hard work, the blood, sweat and tears to learn what they need to successfully fulfill a specialized role. (Ideally 2-3 years before you become an OBM and at least 5 years before coaching.)

I personally made it a goal that I wouldn't coach until I was making at least $80,000 a year and had a successful business.

So, hang in there...your time is coming!

Look, I'm not singing the, "It's so hard" song to scare you. I want to PREPARE you for what lies ahead.

It was easy for me because I was lucky. I had 2 huge wins on my side:

1. I started when the industry was new and there was almost no competition.
2. I had built a strong reputation with in-person networking. Because of that I was easily able to transition into the new business. Not everyone has that luxury.

I've had a lot of jobs over the years. And that's all they were.   J O B S

I went to work, punched a clock, did my time and got a measly paycheck. But deep down it wasn't really rewarding. Never did

I have a job that I could see myself doing for years, even past retirement age.

But being a Virtual Assistant filled that void inside of me. It allows me to nurture my passion of helping others to reach their dreams, while providing income not only for my family, but for my team as well.

When I get emails from clients that tell me I'm amazing, that they don't know what they'd do without me, and so on, that's why I do what I do.

So, while the glamour is a nice bonus to becoming a Virtual Assistant, the ability to help others achieve their goals surpasses all of that.

ACTIVITY: CREATE YOUR WHY STATEMENT

What is Your Why? What brought you to the decision of creating a Virtual Assistant business?

Really think about the honest reasons behind doing this. You will need to hold on to that as you continue on your journey. Especially during the hard times.

Here is my original WHY:

I am a Virtual Assistant first and foremost because I love to help others. I thrive on seeing people achieve their dreams and goals.

It affords me the luxury of being able to be home with my family. I am there for my kids, my husband and my aging parents. I am able to take time for school field trips, to play with my kids, have lunch with my husband or go to doctor's appointments with either of my moms.

I am able to provide a comfortable life for my family financially. We are able to do fun things, have nice clothes and a new car. We are debt-free and can take fun vacations together.

Write your why as if it's already happening.

CHAPTER 4

STARTING YOUR BUSINESS WHILE WORKING A 9–5

Maybe you dream of working for yourself one day or maybe you see layoffs down the road in the company you work for.

Maybe you're starting a family and want the flexibility of working from home or maybe you just know that your current job is not the one for you.

Whatever it was that brought you to make the decision to start a VA business while holding down a 9 to 5 job, you're in the right place.

Becoming a VA is a great way to transition out of a day job.

Many Virtual Assistants begin their business while working elsewhere. I did. And I've never been happier.

It is my recommendation that you do not just decide one day to start a new company and quit your job...especially if it's your only source of income! If you have a spouse or partner that can supplement and the finances work in your favor to quit and go full-time as a VA, great. Just remember you won't be working full-time in the beginning other than on marketing and getting your ducks in a row.

Figure out how much you need to be making to replace your salary and pay for your expenses. Don't undercut yourself here because if you can't make ends meet, you'll be job searching before you know it. Then figure out how many hours you need to work at what hourly rate to make your revenue goal.

Since you probably won't be making that much or have enough clients to fill that many hours right off the bat, plan out a timeline for how long it will take to get there and what steps you'll take along the way. That might include cutting your job back to part time if that's an option to ease the transition.

When you're only working on nights and weekends, it feels like there's an endless list of tasks to set up your business and get clients. Prioritize your limited time for activities that generate income – meeting with clients, getting your name out there, and doing client work.

Limit tasks on building your website and setting up your social media because it can really eat away at your time without accomplishing much to show for it. Don't ignore this completely because both are crucial to your business, but don't spend all your time making sure your website is perfect.

You can always tweak it as you go.

Social media is very important to building your business and while you want to spend quite a bit of time here, it is easy to get sucked in. Schedule time blocks to network online.

Because your time is so limited, it's key that you find places you can get quick answers, ask your questions, and learn as much as you can about how to start a successful VA business. There are many wonderful groups on Facebook that are there to support the new VA.

If you focus on your goal day in and day out, even when you hit rough spots or have a tough day at the office, you're going to start succeeding more quickly than if you think of your business as a side hobby you work on occasionally. Put your all into what you're working toward and keep going. With that mindset, it will become full-time faster than you think.

ACTIVITY: CREATE YOUR PLAN

Spend some time on this.

- ◇ Write down your current list of personal bills
- ◇ Write down your current income
- ◇ Write down a spouse/partner's income

This will help you see how much you truly need to be making in order to make ends meet.

Now figure out:

- ◇ How many hours do you need to work at what rate of pay to make this happen?
- ◇ How long do you project it will take to achieve that level of income?

Example:

Let's say you need to earn $2,500 a month to make ends meet.

At a rate of $25 per hour (standard new VA rate) you would have to work 100 hours per month or about 25 hours per week.

You would need 10 monthly retainer clients of 10 hours per month each to achieve this goal.

It could take 6 months to a year to grow to that number of clients your first year. This is why it's important to grow your skill set quickly. But we'll cover that later. Now you have your plan.

BUDGETING AND YOUR VA BUSINESS

Listen, I get it. Budgets are boring.

But they can also be the difference between your VA business succeeding and failing. They're a crucial component to running your own business, helping you minimize risks, anticipate profits, budget how many hours you need to work, and decide what to charge clients.

Creating a budget isn't a one-time task. This is something that should be done and reviewed monthly.

Estimate the following components for 1 year, and then provide blanks to enter actual results as you go along each month:

Revenue: Estimate income accurately, but err on the side of being cautious. Use last year's numbers, if possible. If it's your fist year and you don't have previous numbers to go off of, then you will create this as you go.

◇ Each month, update your estimates based on previous months' revenue and growth to be more and more realistic.
◇ Start with targets or goals.

Costs: Consider all of the costs associated with earning your revenue estimates, including:

◇ **Fixed Costs-** Fixed costs remain the same, regardless of how much you're working or how much revenue you're bringing in. These might include: technology and office furniture.

◇ **Variable Costs-** Variable costs depend on how many hours you're putting in or how much revenue you're earning like advertising costs or even childcare.

◇ **Profits-**After estimating your revenue and costs, subtract to determine your estimated profit. Then keep in mind what your monthly and annual profit estimates look like.

ACTIVITY: CREATE YOUR FIRST BUDGET

This doesn't have to be super fancy. I generally either do it on a piece of paper or create a table in Word.

Create sections and list:

⋄ Sales & Revenue
⋄ Business Expenses
  • Recurring fees such as Project Management system, Microsoft, Adobe, etc.
  • Marketing
  • Child care (if you are paying for someone to watch the kids while you work)
  • Equipment – if you're leasing or making payments on a computer etc.
  • Classes you are taking or want to take

⋄ Subtract expenses from sales and that's your net profit.

Take it a step further and factor in your personal expenses and income to determine your net personal income.

Use your new budget before making decisions about expenses, especially variable costs to ensure that you have revenue coming in to cover those costs.

You can also use it to project your estimated taxes, if your business is set up in a structure that requires quarterly tax filings...something you definitely need to find out! (U.S. self-employment tax is approximately 13.5% of your net profit.)

CHAPTER 5

BEFORE YOU CAN BUILD A HOUSE, YOU NEED A SOLID FOUNDATION

Getting started on your new business journey is so exciting. It's like dating someone new. Thrilling, adventurous and you just don't know what you'll find when you dig deep. Like dating, you learn what you like and don't like, what works for you and what doesn't and you adjust.

Now that you're ready to take the plunge, you probably feel excited, terrified and overwhelmed.

Where do you start?

What do you need?

Where do you get clients?

Relax. Take a deep breath. I'll help you get there.

Before you can really jump in and begin attracting clients, you want to build your foundation. This was an area I skimped on in the beginning because I didn't know any better. And it cost me money and lost time.

I'm here to save you that headache.

I know you're excited. I know you're ready to jump in and get your feet wet. Remember, Rome wasn't built in a day. They didn't build the Empire State Building from the top, down right?

How many Fortune 500 companies got their start in garages or dorm rooms? Facebook for example. Before Zuckerberg built an immense platform for Facebook, he started with a small platform for connecting old college buddies. The basis.

You need to build your foundation. The nice thing is that it can be done while you work on getting that first client.

Where do you start?

RALLY THE TROOPS

You need to create a support structure within your family and friends circle. Especially your immediate family. They need to understand and be on board with what you are about to do.

Partners/spouses must realize this is not something that will be an overnight success. The money will come, but not right away.

If you're working, you may have to continue working until you can replace your income. But this means long hours and working weekends. Your family needs to be ok with that.

Kids need to know that when you're working, you're working. That's a hard one and an area I still battle after almost a decade. My kids (even the grown-up ones) don't seem to understand that just because I work from home, it doesn't mean I'm not actually working.

Get the family involved in planning so they can be excited and feel like a part of the company.

Kids can be pretty creative...let them help come up with a business name.

Run business ideas by your spouse/partner.

My husband works in the company with me. While it's my business, my name is on all the papers, he's still my partner. I run ideas by him, when I have trouble with a team member or client, we talk about it. We come up with new ideas to be strategic, systematized, and efficient.

He's involved as much as he can be and it makes him feel like he's able to contribute far more than just doing a few tasks here and there.

So, let your family help you build some of the foundation for your business. They will be far more on board and supportive.

PLANT YOUR ROOTS

Where are you going to work? You **must** have a functioning workspace.

Find somewhere that is going to be quiet and free from distraction. I've had several different offices, in several different rooms. I started in the living room. That was not a good place to try and work.

Then, I tried to work in my bedroom and it was better, but I didn't have a whole lot of room in that particular house. I felt cramped all the time.

So, I tried the dining room. It was better, except I had a great view of the kitchen. I was constantly being distracted by dishes, or by laundry. I was right by the door, so the dogs were always wanting to go in and out. It was a main hub, so people were always coming in and out. The kids were coming in and out and wanting something. I was constantly getting distracted.

Finally, I could move into a dedicated office. That was awesome. That was my space. I painted it the way I wanted. I set it up the way I wanted. I made it mine.

Then, when I moved to my current home, again, I tried a couple of different rooms. Hubby and I tried working at the kitchen table. That was difficult. We had to clean up our mess at the end of the day so that we could eat dinner there. It wasn't comfortable to sit at in my office chair. It just wasn't the right fit.
Now, we have a dedicated office area in our new and larger bedroom where we are free from distraction.

I'm not looking at the sink. I don't have to hear if the buzzer goes off on the dryer. It's my space and I spend a lot of time there.

If, where you live, having a dedicated space is not possible, get a room divider. You can set it up behind your area, or around your area, to give you that separation from the other part of the room.

IF YOU BUILD IT

I know Virtual Assistants who don't have a website and swear they can get along just fine without it. And I'm sure they can... temporarily.

In this day and age, if you don't have a website, subconsciously your prospective clients will feel you aren't legitimate; that you're a fly-by-night company and not serious about building a sustainable business.

Your website doesn't have to be fancy. It doesn't have to be huge. To start you just need a few key pages.

- ◇ **Services** (this can be your homepage) - you need a page that lists your services and skills
- ◇ **Contact-** how do they reach you? You need a simple contact page.
- ◇ **About-** who are you? What is your background? You need to give the client a little more to go on.
- ◇ **Packages and Pricing** – There is a lot of controversy around this page. Some have it, others don't. I have a combination of the two. I don't list my VA rates, or my big packages that are custom tailored. But I do have some packages that are set rates for set services and I do list those prices right there on my website.

  You need to decide if you want prices on your site or not. On one hand it lets the prospect immediately see what they can expect to pay you. On the other hand, it could drive away a prospect who is just price shopping, especially as your rates get higher. I prefer to get them on the phone and sell them value
- ◇ **Blog-** eventually as you get more experienced, you can start a blog. This accomplishes several things.

- Google doesn't like stagnant websites. Having a blog makes your website constantly changing and evolving. Google likes that and you'll rank higher in search engines.
- You can begin to position yourself as an expert by talking about various topics and giving prospective clients tips.
- It gives you great content you can chunk up for social media.

Your website is going to undergo several revisions as you gain experience and learn new skills. That's ok. You are looking for a starting point, not a final ending point.

I've revised my website multiple times and have changed my business name 3 times to fit my brand and direction.

You're striving for progress, not perfection. You don't have to spend oodles of time or money on your website right now, but it should look professional and clean.

Look at other VA website for ideas...but do not copy them or plagiarize. Be respectful of the time and energy they have put into building their websites.

HARDWARE

While you don't need to run out and purchase a whole lot of "stuff" for your business, you do need a few key pieces of equipment.

Computer

Yes I know this is a no-brainer and you're probably sitting there saying, "Uh, duh..." I list this because you need to be sure you have a GOOD computer. You need lots of memory and speed. Nothing sucks worse than sitting around waiting for pages to load like you're back in the stone ages on dial-up.

External Hard Drive

I put all my files that I don't use regularly on an external hard drive to free up space on my computer. It's also a good back-up

Printer

Starting out, you'll probably be doing a lot of general admin. This could include typing and printing letters and so on for clients as well as your own business. Get a decent printer that can manage that.

High Speed Internet

Yes this is another DUH moment, but again you can't run a successful business on dial-up. So be sure your internet service is at the fastest speed you can get.

SOFTWARE

There are a few key pieces of software you should have in place to make your life much easier as you grow and begin to manage multiple clients and tasks.

Project Management System

You must have a way to keep track of everything you are doing and the time it's taking to complete each task. In the beginning you might be able to get away with a notepad and email, but that won't last long. You'll soon find you're dropping balls and forgetting things.

There are several types of PM systems on the market. Some are free, others aren't. You will have to test a few to find the one that really resonates with you.

Here are a few of the more popular ones:
- **Teamwork PM-** This is my favorite and a high favorite among other VAs. Teamwork lets you create projects for each client, keep notebooks and really organize and structure everything. It's very user friendly, keeps track of your time and billing. It's what I use to manage over a dozen team members and clients.
- **Asana-** This is another favorite. Anasa lets you create task lists and organize clients. There is a way to track time I believe with a third-party app. Asana has a free version which is why it's very popular.

- ◇ **Trello**–This is the third favorite from what I see others using. I've never actually used it so I don't know much about its features but it will let you keep track of all the work you're doing.

Try several and find the one that really resonates with you. They should all give a free trial so you can get in and play around.

Password Manager

As you get going in your business, you are going to end up with dozens upon dozens of passwords for yourself and for clients. You need some way to keep track of all of them.

I create a notebook in my PM system for each client with their passwords so my team can access them all.

But on my computer and other devices, I use Roboform. It allows me to quickly access logins on all my devices with just a couple of clicks. It's a huge time saver and one that I'm grateful to have learned about early on in my business.

This way, it saves you from having to go back and forth to a binder or an excel sheet every time you need a new log in. It's right there for you.

Last Pass is a newer program that's gaining popularity as well.

Office

You'll need to be sure you have Microsoft Office so you can access Word, Excel, PowerPoint and so on. It's about $10 a month for a subscription and you never have to buy updated software. It just automatically updates from time to time.

Email

Make sure you have a branded email address. Using something like tracey@gmail.com or virtualassistant@gmail.com is not professional. It makes you look like a newbie, and even though you are, you need to put out the persona that you are a very professional Virtual Assistant. So be sure and use an email address that has the same domain as your website (i.e. tracey@ tracey-osborne.com or tracey@daringwomanmedia.com).

Backup

Get a backup system in place. I mentioned the external hard drive and it's great, but it's not what I use for backup. I use Carbonite. It automatically backs my computer up to a remote server every time I change something. This is a crucial piece of equipment. I did not have a backup early on and in my 2nd year in business, my mother board died. I lost EVERYTHING. Pictures of my kids and family, all my client files...everything. I won't be caught without a backup now.

Dropbox

This is a great way to share documents with clients. It's fast and easy to just drop something in a folder and BAM...the client has it. You can also use it as cloud storage, but it does cost money to use so keep that in mind.

KNOW YOUR LEGAL STUFF

Unless you're a law buff, the legal stuff is as dry as it gets. But it's also really important. As a business owner (even if it's a very small VA business), setting up the proper legal protection from the beginning

can mean the difference between getting paid and not, getting in hot water with the IRS or not, and getting sued out of nowhere or not.

These are the basics you need to know and have as a VA business owner.

Contracts

Every, every, every client needs a contract with you from the very beginning. No ifs, ands or buts. They will protect you in the event a client does not want to pay you for work you've performed.

You can find basic, fill-in-the-blank agreements online for contractors, but be sure they come from legitimate legal websites like LegalZoom or Legal Shield. Review them at least annually to make sure they are up to date and reflect your current rate.

I also encourage you to sign up for Legal Shield (also known as Prepaid Legal). Legal Shield allows you to get legal protection from their provider law firms to help you run your business confidently for a low monthly fee. They will review contracts, send emails and answer questions as you get your business started.

Business Formation

Many VA's assume that forming a business is as simple as saying, "I'm open! Send me your work!" But thanks to the IRS, it is more complicated than that.

Did you know there are 6 different ways you can structure your small business? Each has strengths and weaknesses, and some work better for VA and freelancer businesses than others. You can choose what works best for you, depending on how you want to report taxes and how you want to structure profits.

The Small Business Administration outlines the different choices you have so take a look if you want to make sure you're using the best structure for you.

If you're still unsure, talk to an accountant or lawyer.

Business Name

Once you're ready to form your business, you'll need to register it by a company name or under your name with your state. Before doing so, most states require that you do a simple search for existing businesses with the same name.

While you're at it, it would be to your benefit to do a trademark search for your company name, which is a nationwide database to ensure you aren't violating another company's trademarked name.

Website Design

Whether you build your website yourself or you use a contractor to design your website, be careful about the images used. If a photo's copyright is violated on your site, you will be considered liable and could owe the owner regardless of who put the photo there. Some companies have gone after businesses that have violated their copyrights, so make sure you own rights to the photos you're using.

Also keep in mind that photos marked, "Royalty Free" or "Creative Commons" are not necessarily free to use. Buy stock photos from a legitimate stock photo site. They will make the legal stuff easy on you and give you the rights you need in exchange for the cost of the photo.

BOOKKEEPING

Even as a sole proprietor you need to keep track of your income and expenses. You need to file a tax return, right?

Quickbooks

A great software for the small business to keep track of your income and expenses. It can be a bit overwhelming if you don't have an accounting background and not sure where to list what. But you can easily hire someone to set it up and show you how to best use it.

Excel

I used Excel for almost 10 years. It worked for me. I had one page of income for the entire year and then 12 worksheets listing all my expenses in various categories. I just recently switched to Quickbooks as my accounting became more complex.

Talk to an accountant about your best options but be sure you are regularly taking care of the books.

SETTING YOUR OFFICE HOURS

One of the nice things about owning your own business is that you can create your own work hours. Some like to work early in the morning. Others prefer late at night. For me, old habits die hard. I'm an 8-5'er. Well more like 10-4'er (grin).

That's my schedule and when I'm in the office, I'm in the office. This is where I let corporate sink back in and I get into that work mentality. I guess you could say, "I'm in the zone."

In fact, I get downright irritated when I'm in my zone and I continue to get interrupted. I try to keep my distractions to a minimum. Just ask my husband. He works in my business with me and when I'm in my zone, he has a really hard time just getting my attention. And he sits right next to me! I tune out the world.

What does your schedule look like?

If you have younger kids, then you will schedule your day around them. Maybe you work very early for a few hours, then back to it at naptime and again in the evenings.

Or you get the bulk of your work done between 10pm – 3am (I've seen this happen). If it's getting done on time, your clients really shouldn't care.

It is good to put office hours in your contracts so your clients know what to expect and it gives you that feeling of obligation.

Your task if you haven't done this, is to set solid business hours for yourself. Let your clients and family know what they are and hold true to them.

Does this mean you can't make time during office hours for a doctor appointment or something? Of course not. You have that flexibility.

But it will create a certain mindset and you will be less likely to get distracted with laundry and dishes.

ACTIVITY: SET YOUR HOURS

My dedicated office hours will be:

WELCOME PACKET

The Welcome Packet plays an integral role when you first bring on a new client. Your Welcome Packet will clearly spell out your boundaries so there is no question as to how your business operates.

In your Welcome Packet you should have these main components:

- ◇ Warm welcome
- ◇ Office hours
- ◇ How and when to contact you
- ◇ When to expect a response from you
- ◇ Turnaround time for tasks to be completed
  - Also spell out when they should have information to you. **Example**: if the newsletter is to be sent on Tuesday morning, you need all of the copy, images, etc. by Friday.
- ◇ What you need to get started (i.e. logins, etc.) – You can get an Excel spreadsheet for logins at http://www.emfem.me/vabook

ACTIVITY: BEGIN CREATING YOUR WELCOME PACKET

Start listing out the components you need to add to your Welcome Packet. Be sure to add in the items listed above.

CHAPTER 6

WHAT CAN YOU DO FOR YOUR CLIENT?

The million dollar question...where you really need to sit and think for a little bit. What can you bring to the table?

Clients require a wide range of skillsets, and while in the beginning you may not be able to offer all those skills, you can definitely enhance and sharpen the ones you do have.

Why should they hire you?

What makes you different from the hundreds of VAs in the market?

This is the area that really counts. Your clients are depending on you to complete tasks for them so they can grow their business. If they hire you for a skillset you don't have, this will create a lot of headache, frustration and cause everyone time and money.

Getting clear on what you can do and what you can offer is crucial. It not only impacts your day to day client work, but it will also affect the marketing you use on your website and promotions.

Your skills will also be the deciding factor in your pricing.

ACTIVITY: LIST YOUR SKILLS!

Set a timer for 5 minutes.

During that 5 minutes, do a major brain dump of all the skills you have from everything you have done in your past.

Were you a cashier or waitress? That's customer service.

If you were a secretary, you've got tons of skills around being a secretary.

Think about every job you've ever had and what skills you learned from each one.

If you have an old resume lying around, that's perfect. Look at your resume. You probably already have a lot of those skills written down.

Organization skills.

Detail oriented.

Professionalism.

Ability to write.

I'm just throwing stuff out there. If you have some technical skills already, you're ahead of the game, and that's awesome. You can definitely write those down as well.

Stop now, and go do this exercise.

Did you do your brain dump? If you skipped it, GO DO IT NOW. You can't do this next part without it.

If you did your brain dump, kudos! Let's move on.

Now that you've written down your skills, let's take a look at what you've written down.

With each one, ask yourself, "How can I translate this skill to a virtual world?"

Customer support and client care

is a great skill to have. Clients are always needs excellent customer support people. Especially in the internet marketing world. You can create an entire package just around customer support.

Email management

is also very popular. Were you a gatekeeper for the company boss? Helping your clients protect their time is incredibly valuable. Busy entrepreneurs need someone trustworthy and professional to manage their inbox and respond to people. That again could be a stand-alone package.

Managing travel schedules

Many entrepreneurs travel a lot and need someone to help them manage their busy travel schedules; booking flights, hotels, etc.

Event planning

If you have any event organization skills at all, that's huge. You can help a lot of these online people do a lot of online and live events. So you can definitely help out there as well. Not to mention, a lot of times they will pay you to travel and help them at the live events. So, kind of a bonus there.

Research

When an entrepreneur starts to create a new product or service, there's market research to be done. Also, researching potential speaking engagements is a good service to provide.

So those are a few ideas on how you can take your current skills and market them.

Other skills you need but may not have would include:

Organization

You simply cannot be disorganized and make it in the VA world. In order to manage all of the work that will come your way, you have to get organized. If you are not a naturally organized person, fake it 'til you make it!

I wasn't organized in the beginning and it cost me a lot of money and good clients. When the ball gets rolling it moves fast. If you aren't organized you're going to forget things, lose things and ultimately lose clients.

It takes a lot of effort to stay organized if it's not a natural skill, but like anything, if you work at it, then being organized gets easier and becomes a habit.

There are websites and books on getting organized. Do some research here if you need to, but you need to get organized!

An Eagle Eye

You MUST be detail oriented. Nothing ticks off a client faster than getting work back that was not done properly and/or with errors.

> 1. Slow down. It's not a race. Take your time on your work and less mistakes will happen.
> 2. Proof your work! Check for typos. Double check instructions. Test links and opt-in boxes.

If you're not naturally detail oriented, you're in good company. It's something I work at on a daily basis. In the beginning, I handled task work like everything else in my life. I rushed into it. I didn't check my work.

I did not proofread what clients sent. And I made a ton of mistakes because of it.

Learn now to become detail oriented. If you're already there, you have a head start on your competition because I can tell you, it's not easy to find someone with an eagle eye.

Get Technical

You need to learn basic technical skills. You need to learn how to put a blog post on WordPress. You need to learn how to create a newsletter in the various newsletter platforms such as Mail Chimp and Aweber. It wouldn't hurt to have very basic HTML skills so that you can find errors or quickly make a change on something. You don't need to have coding skills. But some basic HTML can help solve problems quickly sometimes. There are some resources in the resource section where you can go and take some online classes and get some of those skills.

Focus & Dedication

Now, you wouldn't think these would not be skills, but they absolutely are. If you can't stay focused while you are trying to work and build your business, and you are constantly being pulled in a million different directions, you're not going to be effective and efficient. If every time your email notification sounds you head for your inbox, or you are constantly checking Facebook, or doing laundry, you are going to find yourself at the end of every day wondering what in the world you actually accomplished. You have to have focus.

CHAPTER 7

SHOW ME THE MONEY!

You can put all the fluff and stuff that you want into your WHY, and while it's true and heartfelt, ultimately, you're here for one main reason...to make money.

What's the one thing that's going to make the biggest difference for your business as a Virtual Assistant?

Hint: It's the same thing that success coaches advise their start up clients to do to ensure success.

DEFINE YOUR NICHE

As you grow, you'll likely expand your niche, but as you're getting started, the best thing you can do for yourself is to get really clear on who you serve best and how.

General VAs can become lost in the sea of competition. They don't stand out enough for anyone to say, "You're the person I've been looking for!"

So, how do you stand out and get noticed?

First, determine what you do best.

If you have not completed the skills activity, do it now.

Think about your work experience, training, and skills. What translates well to being a VA?

Do you dabble in design? Are your communication and customer service skills top notch? Can you build a website quickly and effectively? Are you a proficient writer?

What do you do that people rave about? Is there anything that customers would pay you for and keep coming back to you repeatedly?

Finally, what do you enjoy enough to do over and over again?

That's your sweet spot – you're talented at it, people will pay for it, and you can form repeat business around it.

Identify your passions.

What is that one thing you could do all day and not worry about getting paid? Or that one area you just can't get enough of?

For me, it's health and fitness. I'm a health and fitness fanatic. I love to learn about all kinds of things from nutrition and raw foods to how to become a marathon runner.

I'm also passionate about learning how to build a strong business. I read lots of books and watch webinars, take courses and so on to continue building my skills and knowledge. (Something I strongly advise you to become passionate about too.)

I tend to attract clients who are in the health and wellness industry as well as business minded people such as coaches, internet marketing experts, and so on.

They are who I love to work with most.

ACTIVITY: WHAT ARE YOU PASSIONATE ABOUT?

Identify your top passions. Food, shopping, family, parenting, animals...whatever. List it out.

Looking at that list, you now need to see which might be a viable niche.

You may have to do some research. You need to know if the industry or industries you are leaning toward are profitable.

Are there enough successful people in that industry to support hiring a Virtual Assistant?

For example, I originally wanted to work solely with raw foodists. But after doing some research I discovered there are only a small handful of raw food coaches out there. While I can incorporate that under the health and wellness umbrella, it can't be my main niche.

IDENTIFY YOUR IDEAL CLIENT

Now that you have your skillset and your niche, it's time to identify your ideal client.

By doing this, you will have a better idea of where to look and how to market. It will also make it much easier when vetting potential clients as to whether or not they would be a good fit for you.

Why is identifying your ideal client so important?

Because EVERYTHING you do will be around that client.

Does that mean you can't work with people who don't fall into that category? Absolutely not. It's your choice of course.

Knowing who your ideal client is, will affect how and where you market, what verbiage you use, what words you use, and so on.

Until you have a strong idea of who your ideal client is, you are just throwing spaghetti at the wall and hoping it sticks.

There are three key elements to know in order to attract your ideal client.

1. The ultimate result you provide that TONS of people are wanting.
2. The current problem those people have that make them want that result.
3. The self-identifiable target audience – your ideal client

ACTIVITY: CREATING YOUR PERFECT CLIENT

If you're already a Virtual Assistant with clients, think about your current favorite client. Or think about a favorite boss, leader, or manager.

What is/was it about them that you really loved to work with?

Step 1: List out all the characteristics you liked about those you really love to work with. Was it personality? Work habits? Ethics?

Example:

My favorite qualities:

- Fun
- Creative
- Laid-back
- Intelligent
- Family oriented
- Loves animals
- Strong sense of direction
- Focused
- Loves to teach
- Generous
- Loving
- Goal oriented
- Moral

Step 2: Now conversely, what didn't you like? Think about someone you really did not like to work with. What turned you off?

Example:

My least favorite qualities:

- Micromanager
- Scatterbrained
- No sense of focus or direction
- Lazy
- Abusive
- Too formal
- Know-it-all
- Stuffy
- Disrespectful
- Rule breaker
- Mean

Other Characteristics:

Do you prefer to work with men or women? Does it matter?

How old are they?

What are their hobbies and interests? I like to have clients with similar interests and passions.

Do they have a family? Again, I prefer clients with families. They understand that life with kids happens sometimes.

What is their personality like?

What are their work habits like?

What is their management style like?

How much money do they make?

WHAT PROBLEMS DO THEY HAVE THAT YOU CAN SOLVE?

You need to get to know your target client. You need to learn where they struggle. What areas of business create the most overwhelm for them?

What keeps your ideal client up at night? Not just money. That's an easy one. What problems related to their business or industry would keep them awake?

What fears?

What is more important to them than anything else right now?

What are their greatest challenges?

Where do they get stuck?

How do they feel about not having what they really want?

Make note of any words that seem to repeat themselves. These words are key terms for your ideal client and you need to use them in everything you do. They are the trigger words that will capture your ideal client's attention.

If you don't know the answers to these questions, that's ok. You have some work to do.

Set up some research calls. These are strictly research, do NOT promote yourself on this call unless they as specific questions about your services. Talk to 5 – 10 people in the industry you are looking at.

Tell people you want to understand their needs better. You want to know what they want and what they'd be willing to invest in.

Use pointed questions from up above to get a clear picture of who they are.

What keeps you up at night?

What are your fears?

What is more important to you than anything else right now?

What do you want?

What is keeping you from that?

What are your biggest challenges?

Where are you stuck?

If you could get help with absolutely anything that you'd be willing to invest into, what would it be?

Listen to their answers for patterns. Write down key words, terms and phrases from their responses.

HOW MUCH TO CHARGE?

This is the age-old question. How much should you charge for your services?

As a new VA, you are obviously not going to make nearly as much as an experienced VA.

You can expect to earn $15-$25 per hour for General VA skills.

When you can get more technical skills under your belt, you can increase to $30-35 an hour.

As you get experience and specialize, your rates will increase. Experienced VAs charge anywhere from $45 and up. Specializations will allow you to create higher priced packages.

CHAPTER 8

FINDING THE ELUSIVE CLIENT

Now that you know who you want to work with, how you can help and what you are going to charge them, the next question is, where are they hiding!?!

This can be one of the most frustrating and time-consuming components of building a VA business. There is a lot more competition out there now than there was when I first began in 2008. But even with that being said, there is still more than enough work for everyone if you know where to look.

Friends & Family

when you are first starting, I urge you to tell everyone what you're doing. My rule is, you never know where your next client is going to come from. Tell friends, family, coworkers, the bagger at the grocer story...everyone.

Social Media

This is probably your biggest resource for finding clients.

Facebook

I get a lot of clients from Facebook. But there is a trick.

Don't just hang out in the VA support groups. Yes, there are potential clients in some of them. But you need to be socializing in the groups that interest your client.

Marketing, business, mindset, etc. This is where knowing your target client really comes in handy. When you know their interests and pain points, you will know what groups to target to find them.

Here's the trick: Don't join these groups and start singing, "I'm a VA, hire me!" That's a fast way to get blackballed.

You need to engage. Ask questions. Answer questions. Share stories. Get noticed.

> People don't want to be sold, but they love to buy. ~ Jeffrey Gitomer

You need to create that know, like, and trust factor. If you only post about what you do and try to get people to buy, it comes across as a sleazy, used car salesman and who wants to be like that?

LinkedIn
Same concept as Facebook. Get in the groups your client hangs out in and become noticed. Get engaged.

Twitter
Not as great for finding clients, but still has potential. I originally built my client base on Twitter before it changed and people stopped talking as much. Share articles and retweet others. Begin conversations when you can.

Associations

If you can do this, join the associations that target your ideal client. Or at least follow their social media.

Networking

Offline networking is a blast. I miss it tremendously. If you have the opportunity to join one or two groups, I highly recommend it.

The trick with networking is, when you're talking to people at networking groups, make the conversation be about them. You will be remembered more if you let them do the most of the talking than if you just walk up and verbally puke on someone about what you do.

Get a system in place to follow up on any potential prospect no matter where you found them.

Subcontract

Many VAs get so busy they start subcontracting to newer VAs

to help out. This is a great way to get experience and learn new skills. The VA support groups are a good hunting ground for subcontract positions. Again, the same rule follows. Engage. Don't just sell.

Upwork

Not my favorite platform but a great way to get your feet wet. Remember these platforms are where most of the overseas VAs hang out so competition can be fierce. Also, clients who post on these boards are price shoppers. So, expect to bid lower than your normal rates.

The nice thing is you can secure and work with a client on these platforms for a limited time and then take the relationship off of Upwork and make it solely your own. Then you can slowly raise your rates with them.

I had several clients who were with me for years that started on Upwork. It's not the worst place to get good clients.

SOCIAL MEDIA DOS AND DONT'S

I want to briefly talk about proper etiquette on social media. Let me premise this by saying, Big Brother is watching you. And by Big Brother, I mean potential clients.

They're out there and they're watching.

If your personal profile is public, you can be sure they're checking you out. If they see a profile full of slang, vulgarity, cussing, typos, poor grammar and so on you can bet they will run away as fast as they can.

When people come to my profile they learn about my family, my health and fitness aspirations, my sense of humor and my business. I don't swear much, and when I do I'm not using the F-bomb as if it were a comma.

There has been a lot of debate about swearing on Facebook. In fact, for me it's actually a turn-off to see someone dropping cuss words like it's candy. That is someone I won't work with. So, use the cussing sparingly and for emphasis.

When you are interacting, don't get lazy. Don't talk as if you're texting. One of my big pet peeves is to see posts on Facebook such as: UR, U, Wat u doing? I've not hired VAs for my team because of that.

The most you'll see me abbreviate is something like WTH or sometimes even IDK. But rarely. (If you don't know they mean, "What the heck?" and "I don't know".)

If spelling is not your strong suit, get a dictionary. Use spell-check. Proof what you type. And please, for crying out loud, don't spell a prospect's name wrong. Take a moment and double check before you hit post or send.

I have actually refused to hire someone for my team because they spelled my name wrong. Why? Because that shows me they do not pay attention to detail.

Slow down and pay attention!

Brush up on grammar skills. There are great sites out there that will help in this area.

You really need to come across as polished and professional if you want to be hired by quality clients.

Hard selling in the groups is a no-no. We talked about this previously. Except for promo days, be subtle. When I'm engaging, you'll see me post things such as, "As a seasoned VA of almost a decade, it's my experience that..."

I'm not just screaming, "I'm a VA come hire me!"
I'm putting it out there..."Hey I'm a VA and I'm experienced."

By doing this I generate a lot of interest. People go to my profile and page and then to the website and book a call.

So find a way to be subtle about stating what you do.

CHAPTER 9

SOMEONE WANTS A VA...NOW WHAT?

You see a post on social media about hiring a VA. Or you get an email from a job board for a request for proposal (RFP). What next?

Let's talk social media first.

Here's an ad someone posted that I responded to:

First you want to stand out. So just saying, "I sent a PM," is not enough.

You can see one person was asking questions. That's good, but those questions are really better left for a phone call.

I generally say something like what I did in the example. "Hi NAME (and tag them so they get notified), thanks for your post! I'm sending you a PM so please be sure and check your other folder in case I land there."

By doing this they know to go look for my message. Sometimes I add a bit more so I can attract others who may be looking at comments.

"Hi NAME, I'm a seasoned VA of almost a decade. I'm going to send you a PM so please be sure to watch that other folder in case I land there."

Do something that makes you stand out a bit from all the drones who just say, "I sent a PM."

In your initial message to a prospect, you want to generate interest to get them on the phone with you.

Just saying, "Hi I'm a VA and I'd love to help," isn't going to cut it.

Again, you want to position yourself above your competition.

After you comment on their post, you need to send a very compelling email or message depending upon how they want you to contact them.

It should talk a little about you, but more about how you can help and how they can reach you. This is your initial contact with them and it needs to stand out and **WOW** them.

ACTIVITY: CREATE YOUR SOCIAL MEDIA RESPONSE

I use a general canned response that I can tailor toward each prospect's posts and needs. Here's the template you can use to create your own:

I use a general canned response that I can tailor toward each prospect's posts and needs. Here's the template you can use to create your own:

Hi NAME!

In response to your post in NAME OF GROUP, let me give you a brief background on myself.

Add in 2-3 sentences about your background.

Mention the skills they are looking for.

- Either include a link to your services on your website or include a skillsheet for more skills

How does working with you help your clients?

How can they learn more and contact you?

Example:

Hi XXX! It's great to "meet" you! In response to your post in XXX - let me give you a brief background on me and my company and then you can decide if you want to have a phone call to see if we are a good fit for us handling your webinars.

I've been a Virtual Assistant for almost a decade. My team and I specialize in all things techy – such as creating the webinar funnels, sending newsletters, updating blogs and so much more.

You can get a much more in depth range of our skills here: http://www. businesssolutionsmadesimple.com/virtual-support/

We have set up dozens upon dozens of webinars over the years and can put them together pretty quickly, saving our client's time, energy, money and the hassle. Thus allowing them to focus on creating amazing content and doing what it is they do best.

As mentioned, I do work with an amazing team of US based VAs who assist me and my clients with the work and together we make our clients look as phenomenal as they are.

Working with a team has its benefits - no downtime due to sick days or vacation, work can get done faster, and we have a wide range of skills to handle just about anything that comes our way. (Just to mention a few).

And not to mention, it sounds really awesome for clients to be able to say, "I'll have my team handle that."

As a solopreneur, that can help you look much bigger and more attractive to potential clients.

You can learn more about us at www.businesssolutionsmadesimple.com. When you are ready to schedule a time for us to chat, here's a link to my online calendar to save us both time from going back and forth: www. talktotracey.com

I'm giving them a lot of information, directing them to my website to learn more, and sending them right to my calendar to schedule a time to talk.

I'm taking as much legwork out of their search as possible. **Being mindful of their time**.

CHAPTER 10

THE RFP PROCESS

You put in a proposal to serve as a VA for a potential client and then...crickets.

Nothing.

Nada.

Was it your proposal? Your qualifications? Have they just not made decisions yet?

It happens and if you've done your best and made your initial contact amazing, then you know you've done your best. Sometimes people hire the first person they talk to. Other times they end up being wishy-washy and putting out a post and not hiring anyone.

Who knows what is going on in their world? But there are a few things you can do to try to make your response stand out.

There's nothing worse than an otherwise great proposal from someone that clearly doesn't understand a thing about the client. Do some simple research and read the RFP at least 3 times. You'll be surprised at what will jump out at you that other VAs are missing.

Check the potential client's website for more background information.

If the RFP asks for references, provide the number it requests. If it wants samples of your work, send them with your proposal. Do everything asked of applicants (within reason), or don't expect to get the client. If they require certain skills and you don't have them, don't apply.

When the RFP says to email them, don't send a private message on Facebook. Be sure you read through the posts thoroughly and look for hidden instructions.

When I put out postings for new VAs for my team, I add in hidden instructions.

Example:

> We're hiring again! BSMS is a multi-VA firm that provides very high level quality work to high level business owners. Business is growing and that means the team has to grow too! We are currently seeking a couple technical VA's to handle the overflow. You should have some experience with wordpress, 1shopping cart, aweber, Infusionsoft and how a sales or opt-in funnel operates.
>
> This is great for the newbie who has basic skills and needs guidance on growing those skills, but an eye for detail is key. And you must be able to follow instructions. This is crucial.
>
> Please email your background, references and a couple of web page samples if you have it. Be sure to put in the subject line: I'm a tech VA! This is an as-needed position, we cannot guarantee hours. Pay is $25/hour. Email is tracey@ businesssolutionsmadesimple.com

If I get emails without that subject line, I delete them. If there is no background or references, I delete them. This lets me quickly weed out those who obviously are not detail oriented and don't follow instructions well.

Here's another example:

> I'm in need of helping hands! BSMS is in need of a tech VA (individual preferably) who is knowledgeable in Wordpress, 1shopping cart, aweber, mail chimp, etc. (The basic platforms we use). We also would like you to have basic working knowledge of the steps needed for creating opt-in funnels, sales funnels, etc.
>
> We work in a fast paced environment and while we don't

guarantee hours, there's work to be done and more on the horizon. Please email tracey@businesssolutionsmadesimple. com with the subject line: I'm a rockin' tech! Please include information about your background, your skills and some samples of your work. Also let me know what your all-time favorite project was that you've done in the past.

Sometimes I put hidden instructions in the body. So it might look like:

I'm in need of helping hands! BSMS is in need of a tech VA (individual preferably) who is knowledgeable in Wordpress, 1shopping cart, aweber, mail chimp, etc. (The basic platforms we use). When you respond, let me know what you had for dinner last night. We also would like you to have basic working knowledge of the steps needed for creating opt-in funnels, sales funnels, etc.

We work in a fast paced environment and while we don't guarantee hours, there's work to be done and more on the horizon. Please email tracey@businesssolutionsmadesimple. com with the subject line: I'm a rockin' tech! Please include information about your background, your skills and some samples of your work.

If someone skims the post and just goes straight to the how do I apply part, they might miss or forget that. Again I do it to weed out those who are not detail oriented.

So take your time, create a thoughtfully crafted response and be sure to double check their posts to ensure you've followed their instructions.

Proofread!

This should not need to be said, but unfortunately, it does. Why would they hire someone who allows for typos? Errors will immediately disqualify you, even if you're perfect otherwise. I have personally turned down great candidates for spelling my name wrong. It's all in the details.

I once posted an RFP and one applicant made a funny joke in response to a detail in the RFP. Another told me her problems with my hiring process in her application. Guess who got an interview (and ultimately was hired) and who didn't.

Show your personality if possible and be yourself, as long as you're still being professional.

A great way to do this is to try to connect on social media. Follow the potential client on Twitter or send an invitation to connect on LinkedIn. It shows that you're putting in a little extra effort. Just don't become a stalker!

When you're starting out, small or one-time projects can be a great way to get your foot in the door with people who will hire you again if you do a great job. I've found that around half of one-time projects turn into more work down the road. So don't turn those away in hopes of larger clients down the road.

If you don't have the skills for the client requires, don't apply. You'd be surprised how small the VA world truly is, and you don't want to get a reputation for fudging skills or wasting potential clients' time on interview calls. Plus, the job is going to go to someone more qualified anyway, so it's a waste of your time too.

This doesn't mean skills that are optional or "would be great if you had" or those easy to come by.

If someone needs an Infusionsoft expert and you've never even heard of it, then that's not the right client for you.

Show appreciation for both the opportunity to apply and the potential client taking time to meet with you if she or he does extend an interview. That quick thank you email can be the difference between you and the other qualified candidate!

DON'T JUMP THROUGH HOOPS!

I can't stress this point enough.

A few years ago, I responded to an RFP for an online business manager position. It was a huge company and the opportunity was amazing.

The first thing I had to do was send in a 1-3 minute video talking about myself and how I can benefit their company. It took me 3 hours to create this video. I'd start talking and flub, or the lighting sucked, etc.

That's 3 hours I could have been working on current client work. Or playing with my kids.

There were several steps to this hiring process. I completed them all. In the end it was down to me and one other person and they hired the other person. When I asked them why, they said it was because I wanted to build a large company and they wanted someone who was more focused on just having one or two clients and could really dedicate their time to them.

They knew in the beginning I was looking to build a large company, kept me jumping through those hoops. I spent at least 5-7 hours on that one prospect.

It wasn't all for naught though...I learned that I will never again jump through hoops.

So be leery of any posts that want you to jump through a lot of hoops. You're not a circus performer.

BEWARE THE EMPLOYEE MINDED POST

Sometimes I'll answer these, but most often I won't. Employee minded posts tell me that the potential client is stuck in the employee mindset and will try to treat me as one.
Examples of employee minded questions:

- ◇ Where do you see yourself in 5 years?
- ◇ Why do you feel you would be an ideal fit for my company?
- ◇ What are your strengths?
- ◇ What are your weaknesses?

Example:

I am too honest. I will tell you what I really think and won't sugarcoat it. My clients love the fact that I'm not afraid to express my opinion and not just try to suck up and say I love everything they do.

TRIAL PROJECTS

Now, what if they want a trial project? Great. I have no problems doing trial projects. For example, maybe they want a webinar setup. No problem. I tell them, it takes me this long to set up a webinar, it's going to cost you this much, where do I send the invoice? And I'll do the project.

What you will find, especially if you use Upwork, is people want you to do a project for free. Don't.

If they are not going to pay you to do a trial project, you are not going to do the trial project. And here is why.

These are people who are skilled at getting work done for free. They are "trying people out" doing free trial projects and getting all of their work done for free. They are not actually going to hire anyone. They are just getting their stuff out there, getting it done for free from all these desperate people who need work and want to find a paying client.

They are feeding on the vulnerable.

You do not...I cannot emphasize this enough...**do not do any trial projects for free.**

BARTER CLIENTS

I personally do not barter. I used to. I've tried it in the past. And I always got the short end of the stick because my rates were lower than the client.

For example, I bartered with a wonderful woman, dear friend, who is a mindset coach.

We bartered dollar for dollar. She was charging $150 per hour at that time I was charging $25-$30 an hour. For her one hour, I was spending 5. I got the short end of the deal there.

If you are going to barter, I recommend trading hour for hour. I will give you an hour of my time for an hour of your time. Doesn't matter what the price tag is. Hour for hour straight across the board.

Now I have heard from those who have been successful with bartering, say a website for dental work. I could see where that arrangement could work.

Just be wary and be protective of your time.

FOLLOW UP

I mentioned having a follow-up system in place earlier. This is really important. Potential clients like that. It shows you're on top of things and will be on top of their work as well.

A sample follow-up system:

Day 1 – Be sure they received your RFP

Day 3 – Push for a phone call

Day 5 – Send one final message pushing for a phone call

Day 7 – Move on

**This of course depends on what their responses are and can be adjusted accordingly.

GETTING ON THE PHONE

They've agreed to a phone call! How do you prepare?

Do Your Homework:

⬦ Review their website and learn as much about them as you can.
⬦ Review all messages that were exchanged between you.
⬦ Review the RFP (copy/paste this into a file so you can easily look back and reference it).

Create questions:

⬦ Ask discussion provoking questions.

Make the call about them:

⬦ Listen - Like we talked about in networking, you want the focus on them, not you. People don't like to be sold, but they love to buy. When you listen, you are hearing all kinds of pain points they may not even realize they are exposing.

CHAPTER 11

THEY SAID YES!

They've said yes, now what? Before you hang up and do your happy dance:

1. Review the terms of the contract
2. Set up your initial kickoff call

As soon as you can after the call, (I try to do this immediately) send your contract and their invoice.

Once they sign the contract and pay, send over your Client Welcome Packet.

After a week or so, send a thank you note expressing how excited you are to be working with them. (It's the little things that mean a lot.)

HOW TO GET PAID

Very important. Always request money upfront to avoid getting burned.

There's one exception and that is if you are working as a sub-contractor for another Virtual Assistant. You will most likely not work on retainer when you sub-contract because they can't guarantee hours.

To invoice your clients, PayPal is the easiest way to go. Yes, there are PayPal fees and you need to take that into consideration. You cannot expect your clients to cover PayPal fees. It's a business expense and you should be able to write it off on your taxes. (Check with your accountant to be sure!)

You can use Freshbooks to invoice as well.

I highly do not recommend accepting checks for multiple reasons. It takes forever to get the check and you don't want to start working until that check has been received and cleared. And...checks bounce.

There's also Intuit Merchant accounts. The fees are a little higher than PayPal unless you can get the clients to pay from a checking account in which case it's only $.50 per transaction. That's another option, except it's only valid for US clients and contractors.

WHEN DO YOU INVOICE?

Some people will pro-rate for the month. So let's say John starts on January 7th, they'll pro-rate that month. I personally don't do it that way. If John starts on January 7th, he just gets billed on the 7th of every month. Or I will tell him, we will bill him on the 7th now, and then moving forward, he is going to get moved to either the 1st or the 15th.

He's not losing any time. He still gets his hours, we're just moving the payment dates to be more easily managed.

Definitely make sure you have something in your contract so that if they are more than 5 days late, you cease all work. Don't do any work if you have not gotten paid.

I know some people who let their clients get thousands of dollars into the hole and then got jilted because the client didn't want to pay that large invoice.

Cover yourself and be sure they know that if they are late, work doesn't get done.

KEEPING TRACK OF HOURS PURCHASED/USED

How long do you keep their time on the books? Do you have a "use it or lose it" policy? Or do you roll over?

I personally roll time over for 30 days. If after the 2nd month, I see they are not going to be using their time, I will stop invoicing them and I will talk to them. It could be a matter of them not knowing what to delegate. It could be that business isn't going well for them and they are feeling broke and doing the work themselves.

You may need to adjust the contract for a lower amount of hours.

Sometimes they just don't have enough work to sustain a retainer and they just buy a block of time. If they purchase a block of time, I will usually keep that on the book for about 6 months and then it expires.

CHAPTER 12

CLIENT MANAGEMENT

When you sign on a new client, you need to have systems in place.

This is why we created your contact and onboarding packet earlier.

In your onboarding process, they need to know how to work with you.

When they can get in touch with you?

How are they supposed to send you their work?

When can they expect a response from you?

What do you need to get started?

For example, my clients send me work via email with a couple of exceptions. I have a couple that will call me, real quick calls, or will send me a message on my phone. And that's ok, I expect that. But, they also know that if they message me on my phone and it's before 8am or after 5 pm, they are going to hear about it.

My clients can also reach me on Skype.

Some VAs will actually give their clients access to their project management system and the clients can add new tasks there.

Some clients have their own client management system that they will want you to join. That's ok but it makes a little bit of more work for you, because you have to move stuff into your own project management system so you can track your time.

Honestly though, I rarely come across a client who wants to manage their own PM system.

What is a reasonable amount of time for them to expect a return or to hear back from you?

You should respond to emails the same day, within a few hours or at least by the next day if the email comes in late. If they email you 5:00 on Friday, they should do that knowing they are not going to hear back from you until Monday. My clients know I don't check my email on the weekends and that they are not going to hear back from me until Monday. If they have an emergency they know to text me.

A reasonable turnaround time for getting work done for most tasks is 24 – 48 hours depending upon the task. If they send you a newsletter on Monday, it should be able to be sent out by Tuesday. Of course bigger projects are going to take a little bit longer. But, reasonable expectations should be 24-48 hours.

Be sure they know how soon they should expect to hear from you.

THE SILENT CLIENT

What happens when they don't send work? They've paid for 5 hours or 10 hours and they are not sending anything. Instead of sitting there waiting, reach out to them. Talk to them.

Get them on the phone and ask what's going on in their world. They may not know how you can help, especially if you're working with somebody who's never worked with a VA before. You have to guide them. Get them on the phone and talk to them. Find out what they are doing that they could be delegating.

Sometimes you have to generate your own work. Come up with an idea for them for a teleseminar, or a webinar or a free offer for their website. There's some work for you right there. So be thinking, not just sitting around waiting, twirling your thumbs.

It also makes you look really good in their eyes because you are looking out for their business and how they can grow it.

THE MEANIE

What do you do when a client is just plain mean?
It happens. It's rare, but it happens.

I've had a couple of these over the years.

I've had one in particular that was the worst. She was an online business management client. Things went well for the first month or so. Then all of a sudden, her true self started showing.

I started to get very, very verbally abusive emails…one right after another telling me I don't know what I'm doing. That I need to be researching how to be a better project manager, or more organized.
By the end of a couple of months, she had me believing I didn't know what I was doing, that I shouldn't be doing this anymore. At that point, it was 6 years in my company. I had let one woman brow beat me so badly that I was ready to hang up my hat and just go find a job.

I was at the point where I would get physically ill and feel like I was going to throw up just to check my email. Imagine that. Feeling like you were going to throw up every time you have to go check your emails. And in our line of work we check our email frequently during the day.

What do you do in that case? Fire them. Immediately.

Unfortunately, I stayed as long as I could. The money was awesome. She paid very, very well. She paid on time. And the reason she did was because she went through VAs and OBMs like crazy.

I found out I was not the first person this had happened to. I am definitely not going to be the last person this happens to. I do believe I'm the first person who actually called her out on it. I finally flat out told her she was mean and abusive.

Now I know the second they get that way, I give them one

warning and then they're fired. No notice, no warning. I'm done. I won't tolerate it.

You do not deserve being verbally or emotionally abused. You don't deserve feeling ill every time you check your email because you're terrified of what you'll find waiting for you.

You deserve clients who love and support you.
The next time I had a client who started down that path, I immediately terminated our contract.

Don't keep clients that are mean or are otherwise not a good fit.

If you don't like the work and you don't like their personality, they are not a good fit. It's OK to email them and say, "We are just not a good fit."

As soon as I sent that termination notice, a weight was lifted off my shoulders. That physical sickness feeling left. I didn't care what was waiting for me in my inbox. I had given her a 30-day notice and was very professional and did my time. She sent more emails that told me where I was lacking...but I no longer cared.

Within about a week after giving her notice, I had already replaced her income.

You don't need to keep a mean client just because they pay you well. Or just because they pay you. It is not worth it. It is not worth it to your mental and physical well-being. So, if you get a mean client, dump them.

Dump them quickly.

THE SECRET TO SUCCESS

What if I told you there is one secret to succeeding as a VA that was more important than anything else you could do for your business?

And what if it is also what thousands of companies, from the very small to the Fortune 500, strive to do every day and that you could do it too?

Finally, what if it's so simple you are already trying to do it without it being a real, clear strategy?

So what's this mystery that's so vital to your business' success? Steady, repeat customers.

It's great to get one-off projects, or the client that pops in from time to time. But your business is going to be built on monthly, recurring clients.

From the moment you get a new client, your job is to keep them as a repeat client. That starts with a clear, simple onboarding process and continues with consistent communication.

Nothing ruins the trust faster than a VA who stops communicating because they got behind or made made a mistake.

Consistent, concise communication is key.

Pick up the phone instead of sending an email. Do something special at the holidays. Write them a thank you note for each referral. Take the time to let clients know you personally care about them and you appreciate their business.

Send an occasional card just to say, "Hi, I appreciate you." You want your client to feel special and loved, just as you want to feel that way from your clients.

Be the expert.

Whatever your client is hiring you to do – customer service or general VA stuff, design work, social media, you name it – be the expert. They've got their own stuff to think about, so they are looking to you to know what you're doing and keep them informed.

Stay on top of trends and new products. Chances are your client is hearing about them and will come to you with questions. Continuing education is key.

Clients need to know that you are looking out for them and you have the answer as to whether or not they should jump on the next shiny, new object.

Your invoice is not the place for surprises.

Want to see how fast a client will run? Send them an invoice with extra hours that were unauthorized.

I have actually terminated a VA because she sent multiple invoices with high overages. I'm talking 10+ hours over our agreed upon retainer.

I gave her one warning and the next time it happened, I terminated her for breach of contract. (It is a clause in my contract that overages must be authorized.)

When you send weekly time reports, then clients know when they are about to run out of time. Let them know, "We have 1 hour remaining in the month, do you want me to add overages to your next invoice or send an invoice for another 5 hours to cover it?"

They will be very grateful for the honest communication and the ability to make an informed choice.

I send time updates every Friday for my retainer clients.

If a task or project takes longer than expected, let them know. If they've chatted your ear off for hours and you charge for calls, remind them that they are being charged for the call.

If you've incurred expenses that you're seeking reimbursement for, they should have been preauthorized.

Being honest about time is much better than surprising your client with a huge bill and never hearing from them again.

Create your own work. One word of caution. Heed all of the advice above before employing this technique. Talk to the client as their expert and advise them of opportunities you've found that they might be missing. Let them know the results they can expect and the investment they'll need to make it happen. Once you have their approval, then start working.

CHAPTER 13

WORK AND LIFE – CREATING THE PERFECT BALANCE

This is a very important section. There has to be some kind of a balance between your work and your personal life.

If not, you're going to find yourself either working 16 hours a day or you're going to find yourself goofing off too much and not getting work done and therefore losing money, losing clients, and hurting your business.

There has to be a balance.

You have to create boundaries.

Your family needs to know when they can expect to have your attention and you need to have that precious family time. You also need to have alone time.

Conversely, your clients also need to know when you're available.

If you don't create boundaries, you are going to be pulled in so many directions you won't know which way to go and what to do. Nothing gets done and no one is happy, especially you.

Example, I rarely work on weekends and my clients know this from the start. My office hours are Monday – Friday, 10am – 4pm ET.

There are times I'll work early in the mornings. There are times I'll work late at night. Sometimes I'll even work on the weekends, but it's usually because I'm working on my own products. But my clients don't know this because then they are going to expect me to be responsive during that time.

I had a client text me on Valentine's Day (Sunday) to wish me a Happy Birthday. (My birthday is on Feb. 13 and yes, I expect presents.) But after that he started texting about business and expecting some things done because we are transitioning our relationship to his new in-office assistant.

It's all fine and well that things need to get done, but I had to remind him that not only was it a Sunday, but it's a holiday and I wasn't working. What he didn't know was that I'd actually spent the entire day finishing this book.

He didn't need to know...all he needed to know was that it was a weekend and I would handle business issues on Monday when I was in the office.

Make sure your clients are clear on boundaries...and stick to them! That's equally important. You have to enforce and adhere to your own boundaries. If you don't then why should your clients?

I barely check email on weekends and if I do, I don't respond to client email unless it's urgent. I get a heads up on what to plan for during the week, but I handle it on Monday.

My clients are aware that I don't respond to emails on the weekends and they respect that.

I mention creating office hours several times in this book because it is very important to have them for several reasons.

Your clients need to know when they can expect to hear from you, when you can be responsive to get work done and so forth.

It also helps you focus and get into a working mindset. This helps to limit outside distractions. My poor husband can barely get my attention when I'm in my work mode and he sits right next to me in our office!

You need to make sure you leave time for yourself. My self-time is basically between 8 am and 10 am, when I'm working out and taking care of myself. I also have self-time on weekends to do whatever I want or need to do.

You also need to have family time. That's why I try very hard to leave the office around 4 so that I have that time with the kids. We have limited weekends together because they go to their dad's most weekends, so it's important to me to have that time with them in the evenings and on Saturday mornings before they leave.

It's very, very important that you don't let yourself get so overwhelmed with work that you are relaxing those boundaries and pretty soon you're working 16 hour days, 7 days a week.

When that happens, you will soon find yourself on the fast end of a burnout.

CHAPTER 14

MANAGING THE DAY TO DAY

Life is humming along smoothly. Client work is pouring in and all is well with the world. Or is it? Chances are, you're feeling incredibly overwhelmed and at the end of the day nothing is getting done.

We all have the same 24 hours in a day. It's what we do with it that really counts.

Have you ever wondered how successful people can get done everything they do? The meetings, the paperwork, the management, this, that and the other thing.

And then there's you.

At the end of the day you sit and wonder, where in the heck did the day go? And why did I sit here working for 8 hours but feel like I haven't accomplished a darn thing?

I have two words for you. Time Management.

Being a successful Virtual Assistant means juggling multiple clients and tasks. Clients want, and quite frankly, expect their work to be done in a timely manner...and it should be.

But if you are spinning your wheels every day and going nowhere fast, you'll soon find yourself in a heap of trouble and working 16 hour days to get caught up.

Getting behind is not a fun feeling.

So what's a VA to do? Let's look at your day.

TIME MANAGEMENT

Does any of this ring a bell? This is how my day used to flow:

Get up, get the kids off to school.

Sit down to check email, realize the laundry needs done. Get the laundry started. Answer a few emails, and oh wow...look at that pile of dishes in the sink.

OK dishes are done. NOW I'm going to work.

Great, the dogs want out. Get up and let the dogs out.

Oops laundry needs swapped over now.

OK back at my desk. Get a few things done. I wonder what's going on over on Facebook. I better check.

An hour later, ok I've really got to focus now.

'Oooo' a new email, I wonder what that is! Oh, it's just spam. OK I have to buckle down.

Oh let me just change the laundry over real fast and then I will buckle down.

Man I'm hungry. I better eat.

As long as I'm taking a break I'll peek at Facebook again.

OK let's get this newsletter out.

Wow the kids are home already? How did that happen?

Rinse and repeat.

Do you see how you can get sucked into mismanaging your time pretty quickly and not even realizing it's happening?

In the scenario up above, my office was in the dining room. It was in the hub of the house and I was constantly distracted and my

Do you see how you can get sucked into mismanaging your time pretty quickly and not even realizing it's happening?

In the scenario up above, my office was in the dining room. It was in the hub of the house and I was constantly distracted and my attention was pulled away from what I really needed to be doing.

Now my office is in my bedroom. Away from all distractions. (Except my husband's snoring.)

I have set times the dogs go out each day. The dishes are handled before I go to work and same with laundry.

Once I sit down to work, I shut out the rest of the world. But that took a lot of practice. I still have my time sucks, and I'm aware of them and have made changes there as well, but I'm getting off on a tangent. We'll talk about all that in a minute.

SCHEDULING YOUR DAY

How do you structure your work day?

There are several ways to set up your day to be incredibly productive.

Some VAs will block out chunks of time on their calendar based on a task. For example, all newsletters will be done from 10am – 2pm. Then from 2pm – 3pm is blog posts.

They group all of their clients together based on similar tasks.

Others will set certain times they work on each client.

Example: From 10-11 I will work on Bob and then from 11-12 is Mary.

Personally, I've tried both. They don't work for me. But they might for you, you have to play around with it and see what works best.

So how do I structure my day?

Here's my basic schedule:

6:30am – up and walk dogs
6:45am – kids get up and get ready for school
7:50 am – kids get the bus and I'm out the door to workout
8:15am – 9:15am – workout
9:30am – 10am – breakfast and shower
10am – 10:30 – check BSMS emails and BSMS project management
10:30 – 11am – customer support for client
11am – 11:30am – client work
11:30 – 11:40 – walk dogs
11:40 – 1pm – client work (I usually grab lunch in here but I am the kind who eats at my desk while I work)
1pm – 1:30pm – check emails
1:30-3pm – client work
3pm – 4pm – final email check for all emails and project management

Now is this set in stone? No. It's a guideline. Some days emails take longer, other days they don't.

And for me, because I have a team, client work doesn't necessarily mean doing tasks. I do other things and have phone calls during that time frame.

But you can see where I have a pretty structured dan and this helps me to get as much done as I possibly can.

ACTIVITY: HOW CAN YOU BETTER STRUCTURE YOUR DAY?

Some of you are reading this thinking, I'm more of a fly by the seat of my pants kind of gal/guy. I used to be as well. And there's nothing wrong with that, but in the world of being a VA, you have to have some kind of structure in place.

I used to just wing it and do what needed doing as it came in. I told everyone, "Sure I can get that done right away." Not realizing all the other stuff I had promised that was on my plate too.

Next thing I knew, balls were being dropped, clients were getting angry and I was working 16 hour days and hating what I was doing.

Structure is very crucial to managing your time well. Once I created more structure in my day, I found I actually liked it. It's nice to not be frazzled because you over promised and under delivered.

Create a structured day and see how it works for you.

TURNING YOUR TO-DOS INTO TA-DAS!

Create your activity list! Otherwise known as a to-do list. I like to create them the night before and that way I know what I'm doing when I get to the office the next morning.

Prioritize your tasks either in order of importance or difficulty.

I like to put approximately how long it will take to complete each task so I can be sure I'm sticking within my business hours. This also allows me to build in some contingency time for those unexpected items that are sent over and must be done last minute.

Creating a daily to-do list will allow you to see if you are taking on too much of a work-load, or not giving your clients a reasonable turn-around timeframe.

Another idea is to create a master list for the entire week on a Sunday. This lets you see what you have that is recurring, and where you can fill in with work. It will also allow you to give clients a more reasonable turnaround estimate and be able to refuse work if you're too busy. (It is ok to say no.)

I will generally take my list from my Teamwork and export it, especially since I work in multiple accounts. Plus, I like to be able to manually cross off things as I get them done, plus I have a tendency to email myself things that I've forgotten or just thought of to add to my list.

ACTIVITY: CREATE YOUR ACTIVITY LIST.

Create your activity list for the week as best you can. Leave room for last minute projects. Be sure to put an estimated amount of time for completion next to each task.

Example:

Bob's newsletter – 45 minutes
Create webinar funnel for Mary – 2 hours
Set up email broadcast for Dave – 30 min

E-MAIL MANAGEMENT

This is another area we can get lost in because the majority of us communicate with our clients solely via email.

Again, schedule this in your day. Turn off the notifications so you don't get a popup or a sound every time you get an email. I promise the world won't end if someone has to wait an hour to hear from you. If it's an emergency, they can pick up the phone and call you.

Have your email set up in a system. Use folders and filters.

Most of you should be able to get through an email session in about 15 minutes or even less. I personally manage over 10 different emails so there's a bit more for me to get through in each session, but I still can get through a session in about 20-30 minutes at a time.

By having rules and filters set up, you can sort through your inbox pretty quickly.

Assess what's urgent, and what can wait. Handle the urgent stuff immediately. If it can wait, such as reading a newsletter, or responding to a friend, then let it wait.

Don't let your inbox control you.

ACTIVITY: FIND YOUR TIME SUCK

To find out where you're losing time the most, try this exercise. For 2 or 3 days, I want you to keep a journal of everything you do during your work day. Set a timer for 20 minutes. After it goes off, write down what you've done during that time block and how long it took and reset your timer.

You will be amazed at where you're losing precious time.

CHAPTER 15

WHEN THE GOING GETS TOUGH

What do you do when it starts to get hard? By hard, I mean you're working 16 hours a day, it doesn't seem like you are ever going to get caught up and you're really starting to hate life.

It's going to happen. We all get there at one point or another.

So what do you do when it gets there? You just wake up one day and think, "I don't want to do this anymore. I'm done. I'm up at 4am, I'm working until 11pm and I am just tired. I haven't had a day off in weeks."

First thing you need to do here is assess why this is happening.

The number one reason we get into overwhelm is taking on more than we can chew.

A very common mistake most VAs make in the beginning, is to say, "Yes," to everybody. Heck, even seasoned VAs can fall into that trap too.

Saying 'yes' is addicting. Getting new clients is a great feeling. But you have to be very realistic. You only have 24 hours in the day and an even smaller number of business hours. How are you going to choose to use them?

Take a day off. Saturday or Sunday, or even a day during the week, take a day off and go veg on the couch. Do something. Go out with your family. Just take some time for yourself. You need to get some downtime in before you get sick.

Sit back and take a good hard look at your business. And ask yourself, "Am I being realistic in taking on this work-load?"

I've been there a few times. I was saying yes to everything, but for me, it wasn't that I was saying yes to too much, I was saying yes to too much too soon. I had false expectations of what I could do.

I wasn't being realistic with myself about how long it would take me to get things done and trying to get everything done the same day instead of telling my clients it will take 24-48 hours. This is where the realistic expectations come into play.

I also wasn't managing my time well, I didn't make my activity list, I ran to my inbox at every ping, and I had little structure to my day. It wasn't long before I was working 14-16 hour days and not even getting remotely close to being caught up.

When one gets to this point, it's common to play ostrich, burying our head in the sand. The VA stops communicating with clients.

They don't respond because they're behind and ashamed. At this point, they're dropping the ball and turning in sloppy work.

So when this hits you, take a good hard look at where you are. Really analyze what led to being overwhelmed.

Why are you in this position?

Is it that you are just taking on too much that needs done immediately and you're not setting realistic expectations for yourself?

Or is it that you have taken on too many clients?

If you have taken on too many clients, then take a good long look at who your clients are and who you can let go of; people who are paying too little, clients who you have to chase for money, those you don't like to work with, or you don't like their work, etc. Start culling down some of your clientele.

Second and very important is communicate with your clients. Be very honest with them.
I would much rather my team members come to me and admit they bit off more than they could chew, rather than just drop off the face of the planet.

So be very candid. Explain you took on too much and give them a production schedule for their work.

Then tell them you are implementing a new system to ensure this doesn't happen again, and that you will be giving a 24-48 hour turnaround time from here on out.

Spread out the workload over a couple days if you can. In the meantime, don't take any more...if they send you any work, tell them you can't do it now but will get it done on XX date.

Your clients, most of the time, will be very understanding (but a little irritated so expect that). However, they should be very grateful that you came to them and you were honest with them.

For me, for example, if I have a team member who admits to overwhelm, I work with them. I look through their workload and see what I can either reassign, do myself or change the due date. I work with them to ease that overwhelm.

Then we will talk about how it happened. Sometimes it's because I'm not being realistic and giving them too much, too soon.

Your clients may be doing the same thing and not realizing it.

Talk to your clients and let them know what's going on. Be sure to tell them how you are going to change things going forward so this doesn't happen again. They want to hear you admit that you are human and that you are taking responsibility for your actions. Then, they want to hear how you are going to fix this and how are you going to make sure this never happens again.

More often than not, this will strengthen your relationship as long as it's not a continuing issue.

If I have a team member who stops communicating and work isn't being done, I remove them from my team. I cannot stress enough how important open communication is with your clients.

It just recently happened. I discovered my social media manager had stopped posting for almost 2 weeks. I sent multiple emails with no response. So, I simply removed her from my team and sent a final termination notice. I never heard from her as to what happened.

I SCREWED UP!

What happens when you screw up? And you will screw up.

We all do. After almost a decade, I still make mistakes. I send emails with typos, a bad subject line. It happens, we're only human. We aren't superheroes.

Own it.

Take responsibility.

Your clients don't want to hear excuses. They don't care. They're angry. They want to know that you know and understand and accept responsibility for the fact that this happened.

Number two, they want to know it's going to be fixed. So be very clear on how you are going to fix whatever happened.

Number three, what steps are you going to take to make sure this never happens again?

Very, very important...Do NOT stop communicating with your clients when a mistake happens. Yes they may be upset, depending on how bad the error was.

I've emailed clients with an error, what happened, how I fixed it, what steps I'll take to be sure it doesn't happen again, and the response I got was, ok thanks for letting me know.

When you stop communicating with your clients, they panic. They will freak out. They will get angry. And they will fire you.

Let me tell you about a mistake I made once in my 2nd year of business.

This is probably the biggest mistake I've ever made. I was in total overwhelm. I was getting up at 4:00 in the morning and working until 10-11:00 at night. I ate all my meals at my desk. I barely had any time to deal with my children. I was just in complete and total overwhelm. I had taken on way more than I could chew.

So one day I sent out an email for a client, it was supposed to go to a certain list to those who purchased the replay of a call.

I was in a hurry and I did not check my work. I sent it out to her **entire list**.

Thankfully she caught the mistake as soon as she saw the email and contacted me. I freaked out. I thought I was going to throw up because I was so sick over that mistake.

She was furious, but we worked together to fix it. We put a password on the page so that people had to have a password to get to that page, and we sent an email to the whole list letting them know the email was a mistake, the page is password protected and they are welcome to purchase the call.

Then, we sent out an email to the people that had purchased it and gave them the password.

However, it doesn't mean a few people didn't get over to it before we were able to get it all set up, because it took us about a half hour. So she probably lost a little bit of money on that.

What did that cost me? It cost me money, I was on a retainer with her and cut my invoice in half to make up for that plus the other mistakes I kept making because I was so overwhelmed.

Most importantly though, it cost me her trust and eventually it cost me the client.

What did this teach me? It taught me several things.

First, it taught me my method for recovering from mistakes.

I learned to own my mistakes and accept responsibility. Prior to that I was always trying to find an excuse.

I helped to make it right.

I put systems in place immediately to make sure it never happened again. To this day, I will not send out an email unless I have checked the list 3 or 4 times. Every once in a while, a subject line or something will go out wrong, or there will be a typo in there. But as far as which list it's going to, I am very, very careful about that because I never want to make that mistake again.

When you make mistakes, they are learning processes. They are truly only mistakes if you don't learn and grow from them.

Of course, immediately after you make a mistake you're going to feel terrible. And possibly cry if it's a big enough error. I know I have.

Go ahead. Give yourself permission to be upset for a few minutes.

After you've calmed down, stop and ask yourself, "What can I learn from this, how can I make this better, and how can I make sure this never happens again?"

CHAPTER 16

GETTING SUPPORT AND MENTORING

There are many benefits of being a Virtual Assistant and running your own business... **financial freedom, flexibility, and time to enjoy your family and friends** to name only a few! But there are also pitfalls and challenges that can be difficult to overcome on your own.

Let's face it, the VA industry is "virtual" and there is no one in the next office over to ask questions, bounce ideas off of or share experiences!

Whether you are just getting started as a VA or are a seasoned VA who wants to take your business to the next level, **working with a mentor and a seasoned pro can help you get to the next level** in your business!

There are many free support groups on Facebook, but there's a lot of noise and you aren't guaranteed any actual "coaching" from them, but they are great to join regardless.

If you are serious about creating a strong, sustainable, and successful Virtual Assistant business, you want to work directly with a coach or mentor. Someone who has been there, knows what it takes to create a viable business and can guide you in the right direction.

I remember all too well that when starting out as a VA, money is tight and one-on-one coaching may not be an option.

I left my position as Vice President of a finance company to spend more time with my young daughters, start my own multi-VA business, and have control over my time and income.

I know EXACTLY what it's like to be a small business owner and be cash strapped and time poor.

There were times I wanted to quit.

Times I thought I had made a mistake.

And times when I felt so alone.

It doesn't have to be that way for you!

I persevered and now, almost a decade later, I have built a 6-figure multi-VA firm!

My goal with this book is to give you the tools and tips you need to get started and build your foundation. But this book just covers the tip of the iceberg.

As the days go by, and you begin to do the work, whether it's getting your business up and running, securing your first client or working with clients, there are going to be more and more questions pop up.

Even the most experienced business people have coaches, mentors and advisors helping them along the way. No one person knows everything. And when it's your business, sometimes you're just too close to be objective.

Coaching can be expensive, especially when you're starting out. While it's worth every penny with the right person, when you're just getting your VA business started, money is going to be tight...but the need will still be there for help.

Finding the right coach or mentor is crucial and you may test out one or two before you find the right one.

Here are some factors to consider when looking for a coach:

- ◇ They are successful
- ◇ They are very familiar with the Virtual Assistant industry

⋄ They have been in business at least 3-4
    years
⋄ They are well versed in internet marketing

There are a lot of wanna-bes out there who have been a Virtual
Assistant less than a year and then think they can coach. Do your
due diligence and homework.

Remember–

IT'S ALL ABOUT YOUR

success!

ABOUT THE AUTHOR

Tracey Osborne is a woman on a mission. As the CEO of Daring Woman Media, Tracey is determined to make a difference in as many lives as she can...by empowering women on a global scale to unleash their inner strength and let their voices be heard.

In December 2017, Tracey decided it was time to answer the calling that had been tugging at her core for the past few years.

She took a leap of faith and created Daring Woman Media; a publishing and media company where women can share their stories of inspiration, heartache, love and experience, to give someone else the hope, knowledge and motivation they need.

Tracey is the host of The Daring Woman podcast, a weekly podcast that showcases inspiring women who have beat the odds, overcome the challenges life has thrown their way and created powerhouse businesses.

Learn more at www.daringwomanmedia.com

Made in the USA
Middletown, DE
03 March 2019